HOW TO PASS FROM CURSE TO BLESSING

DerekPrince

HOW TO PASS FROM CURSE TO BLESSING

HOW TO PASS FROM CURSE TO BLESSING

Copyright © 1986 Derek Prince Ministries-International

This edition 2014, Derek Prince Ministries - UK
Kingsfied, Hadrian Way, Baldock, SG7 6AN, United Kingdom

Printed by Derek Prince Ministries

ISBN 978-1-78263-116-3
ePub 978-1-78263-145-3
Kindle 978-1-78263-146-0
Product Code T138EN3

Unless otherwise noted, all Scripture quotations
are taken from the New King James Version (NKJV),
© 1979, 1980, 1982 by Thomas Nelson, Inc., Publishers.
Used by permission.

Cover Design: DPM-Asia/Pacific

www.derekprince.com

Contents

Introduction

As I travel and minister in many parts of the world I notice that there are two main responses to supernatural phenomena. The Western world has for so long been influenced by the rational, scientific approach that most people find it difficult to accept anything beyond what can be received through the five senses. It is an unfamiliar idea to many that there is a supernatural dimension that can influence their everyday lives for good or for evil.

On the other hand, virtually everywhere in the non-western world, whether it be in large cities or rural villages, the vast majority of people are well aware that the existence of the supernatural dimension is no theory. While such an awareness is better than ignorance, many still live in fear of having to deal with these realities on a daily basis. In a positive sense this can also mean that such people are also very open to the power of God to bring release from bondage.

I believe that this message of how people can pass from curse to blessing can be of tremendous help to many people, wherever they live and whatever their background. I have proved this over many years. This message has the power to change lives, communities, churches, even whole nations.

I believe there are many people who are fighting something in their lives that they don't fully understand. Every time they are about to succeed, something seems to intervene and keep them from success. Something holds them back from being a complete person, from being completely free, from being able to serve the Lord victoriously as they wish to. They may have never diagnosed it or fully come to grips with it but I believe that the problem they are fighting with is that there is a curse over their life.

This book will show, from the Bible, how curses operate, where they come from, how people can be set completely free and be able to enter in and enjoy the fullness of the blessing that God has always intended for them.

PART 1

The Reality of Blessings and Curses

Are you continually frustrated by sickness, financial pressure or strained relationships? Do accidents regularly happen to you and your family? Do you wonder why some people seem to get more than their share of success and fulfillment?

I believe there are two forces at work in every life: blessings and curses. One is beneficial, the other harmful. To enjoy the benefits of God's blessings and be protected from curses, we need to understand how these forces work.

A curse is not a superstition from the Dark Ages. I will draw on real life experiences of people who were astonished to discover that they were not the victims of blind chance or even heredity. A curse could be described as a long, evil arm that rests upon you with a dark, oppressive force that prevents the full expression of your personality. It may have its source in your lifetime or go back to a previous generation.

01 | How God Changed My Thinking

I was not always as convinced as I am now regarding the reality of blessings and curses. I knew that they were biblical concepts but I was not fully aware of their significance. An incident that God used to change my thinking happened quite a few years ago.

I had just finished preaching in a Presbyterian church in America when I noticed a family — father, mother and teenage daughter. The Holy Spirit seemed to say to me, "There is a curse over that family." There was no natural reason to think this so I went up to the father and said to him, "Sir, I believe God has shown me there is a curse over your family. Would you like me to revoke that curse and release you from it in the name of Jesus?" Immediately he said, "Yes."

I said a short, simple prayer and although I had not touched any of them, there was a visible, physical reaction in each of them when I broke the curse. Then I noticed that the daughter had her left leg in a cast from above the thigh to the bottom of the foot. I asked the father, "Would you like me to pray for the healing of your daughter?" He said, "Yes, but you need to know that she has broken it three times in the last eighteen months and the doctors say it will not heal."

Today if I heard something like that, I would know that there was a curse over the family. I prayed a simple prayer. Shortly afterwards the mother wrote thanking me for what had happened. She said that when they went back to the clinic, the X-ray showed that it had healed and she was soon out of the cast.

As I meditated on the experience, I realized that God had shown me there was a curse over the family and led me to break the curse before He permitted me to pray for the healing of the daughter. Why?

My conclusion was that she could not have been healed until the curse was revoked. In other words the curse was an invisible barrier that kept her from the blessings that God wanted her to receive.

Then God began to deal with me about this whole matter of blessings and curses. I was amazed at how much the Bible has to say about the subject.

However, generally speaking, it is seldom mentioned in sermons.

An incident in my own life further emphasized the reality of this invisible realm. In 1904 one of my grandfathers had commanded a force in the British army that was sent to China to suppress the Boxer Rebellion. He brought home some pieces of Chinese art which, over the years, became family heirlooms. After my mother died some of them passed to me.

The most interesting items were a set of four beautifully embroidered dragons which we hung on our living room wall. About this time I began to sense some opposition to my ministry but I could not identify its source. It was manifested in the form of various frustrations, financial hindrances, disappointments and communication problems.

"...the curse was an invisible barrier that kept her from the blessings that God wanted her to receive."

Eventually, after a period of intensive prayer and fasting, I began to notice a change in my attitude towards the dragons. I asked myself, who in the

Bible is represented as a dragon? It was clearly Satan.
I began to realize how inappropriate it was for me
to have such things on the wall and so finally, as a
simple act of obedience, I got rid of the dragons.

In the months that followed there was a dramatic
improvement in my personal finances. As I
meditated on the experience I received fresh insight
into Deuteronomy 7:25-26 where Moses warned
Israel against having anything to do with the idolatry
of the nations of Canaan.

> *You shall burn the carved images of their*
> *gods with fire; you shall not covet the*
> *silver or gold that is on them, nor take it*
> *for yourselves, lest you be snared by it; for*
> *it is an abomination to the Lord your God.*
> *Nor shall you bring an abomination*
> *into your house, lest you be doomed to*
> *destruction like it, but you shall utterly*
> *detest it and utterly abhor it, for it is an*
> *accursed thing.*

In bringing this image of a false god into my house,
I had unknowingly exposed myself and my family
to a curse. How grateful I was to the Holy Spirit for

opening my eyes to what was involved.

I began to see a principle connecting the improvement in my personal finances and the healing of the girl with the broken leg. In both cases the curse was like an invisible barrier. With the prayer of release came healing and, in my case, financial prosperity.

Let me share one other experience that vividly illustrates the reality of blessings and curses. Once when I was in South Africa I met a Jewish lady who I'll call Miriam. She is a believer in Jesus, saved and baptized in the Holy Spirit. She was a very highly qualified and well paid executive secretary. As a result of answered prayer she found herself working for a man who was the president of his own business. She soon discovered that he, along with all the company executives, were in some strange cult led by a prophetess.

After a little while, her boss said to her, "Our lady guru has pronounced blessings over us and we would like you to type them out for us." However, Miriam soon discovered that they were anything but blessings. As a committed Christian she explained to her boss that she didn't feel free to type them. He was very gracious and apologized for not realizing it would go against her conscience.

However, almost immediately after, Miriam's fingers in both hands curled up and became absolutely stiff. She couldn't bend them at all and so she couldn't work. The pain was so agonizing she couldn't sleep. The doctor diagnosed it as rheumatoid arthritis.

A Christian friend of Miriam's who had heard my messages "Curses, Cause and Cure", played her the three cassettes to the point where I lead people in a prayer of release from any curses over their lives. Suddenly, for no natural reason, the cassette completely jammed and wouldn't even eject.

Up to this point Miriam had been quite sceptical and had only listened to please her friend. However eventually Miriam agreed to read out the printed version of the prayer of release which her friend happened to have with her. By the time she had finished reading it her fingers had completely freed up and the pain was gone.

The same doctor examined her again and confirmed that she was completely healed. Remember, there had not been any specific prayer for healing, only the prayer of release from a curse.

Whatever our background, it is vitally important for us to realize that this whole realm of blessings and curses is not some primitive superstition left over from the Dark Ages. It is very real and God wants His people to have a clear understanding of such matters so that we may live in victory, experiencing the full blessing of God.

02 | How Blessings and Curses Operate

The operation of blessings and curses in our lives is neither haphazard nor unpredictable. On the contrary, both of them operate according to eternal, unchanging laws. There are two kinds of forces that shape history: visible and invisible. It is the interplay between these two dimensions that determines the outcome of events. If we only focus our attention on the things that are visible and natural we will often be unable to explain why certain things happen the way they do.

We all feel at home in the natural, physical world because that is what we are familiar with on a daily basis. Many people are not aware of anything more than this. However, the Bible opens up another, invisible dimension which is not physical but spiritual.

Paul speaks of both of these dimensions in 1 Corinthians 4:18:

> *We do not look at the things which are*
> *seen, but at the things that are not seen.*
> *For the things that are seen are temporary,*
> *but the things which are not seen are*
> *eternal.*

Natural things are not lasting; it is only in the invisible realm that we can find true and abiding reality. It is here that our destiny will be formed.

Both blessings and curses belong to the invisible, spiritual dimension. They carry supernatural, spiritual power. Blessings bring good, positive results while curses produce bad, negative results. Both are important themes in the Bible.

Two important features are common to both. Firstly, the effects of both blessings and curses can often go beyond just the individual person. Other family members, their community, tribe or even a whole nation can also be affected.

Secondly, both blessings and curses can continue on from one generation to the next until something is done to cancel their effects. This of course has important practical implications. A person who is experiencing the effects of either blessing or curses may not easily discern where it comes from, because its origin may be in the past, even hundreds of years ago.

Once when I was teaching on this in Adelaide, Australia, a lady wrote me a letter afterwards. Her ancestors were from Scotland, from a clan called Nixon. She had historical evidence that as a result of clan wars between the Scots and the English in the 16th century, the Bishop of the Church of Scotland had put a curse on the Nixon clan. She realized that four centuries later, things were happening in her family which could still be traced back to that curse.

"...it is only in the invisible realm that we can find true and abiding reality."

Blessings and curses are words that are charged with supernatural power — maybe the power of God, maybe the power of the devil — but they are words which have an impact on people's lives and can even determine their destiny. Not only that, their effect can continue on from generation to generation.

However, I want to make it very clear that if you are experiencing the effects of a curse, God has already provided the solution for you. You do not have to continue suffering from the effects of it. But first, let me give more of an overall picture.

God as the Source of Blessings

God is the sole and supreme source of all blessings, although they may come to us through many channels. The first time we see blessings operating in the Bible is in Genesis 22 where Abraham had just been willing to offer up his son Isaac in response to the Lord's requirement. At the last moment the Lord provided a ram to be offered instead of Isaac.

> *Then the Angel of the Lord called to Abraham a second time out of heaven and said: "By myself I have sworn, says the LORD, because you have done this thing and have not withheld your son, your only son, in blessing I will bless you and in multiplying I will multiply your descendants as the stars of the heaven and as the sand which is on the seashore; and*

*your descendants shall possess the gate of
their enemies.*
*In your seed shall all the nations of the
earth shall be blessed, because you have
obeyed my voice.*

Genesis 22:15-18

It is very important to notice the reason for the
blessing — because Abraham obeyed God's voice.
That is the basic reason for the blessing of God.
Notice too that the blessing was going to be on all of
Abraham's descendants.

Later on, when Isaac was an old man,
Genesis 27 records how he blessed his son Jacob.
But the strange thing is that Isaac thought he was
blessing Esau, who was his firstborn son. Esau had
gone out hunting venison which Isaac wanted to
eat before pronouncing the blessing. Isaac's wife,
Rebekah, saw an opportunity to take advantage of
the situation for Jacob, their younger son who was
her favourite.

To deceive Isaac (who was blind) she dressed
Jacob in Esau's clothes and even wrapped goatskin
around his neck and arms to appear like Esau who

was much hairier than Jacob. She cooked some young goat's meat just the way Isaac liked it. Jacob pretended to be Esau and took it to his father. Isaac checked his identity by asking him, "Are you really my son Esau?" Jacob said he was; he told a lie. Isaac was convinced so he ate and then pronounced the blessing,

> *Surely the smell of my son*
> *Is like the smell of a field*
> *Which the LORD has blessed*
> *Therefore may God give you*
> *Of the dew of heaven*
> *Of the fatness of the earth*
> *And plenty of grain and wine.*
> *Let peoples serve you*
> *And nations bow down to you.*
> *Be master over your brethren,*
> *And let your mother's sons bow*
> *down to you.*
> *Cursed be everyone who curses you,*
> *And blessed be those who bless you!*

Genesis 27:27-29

Understand that the blessing was tremendous in its

scope and it went on from generation to generation.

A little while later, in comes Esau with the venison which he tries to offer to his father. Isaac realizes that he has been deceived and has blessed Jacob instead of Esau. But note Isaac's reaction,

> *Then Isaac trembled exceedingly and said, "Who? Where is the one who hunted game and brought it to me? I ate all of it before you came and I have blessed him — and indeed he shall be blessed.*
>
> *Genesis 27:33*

Isaac thought he was blessing Esau but he knew the words didn't come from himself. It was a prophetic blessing and because it was prophetic he couldn't unsay it. So Jacob got the blessing and Esau didn't.

I want you to see the nature of blessing, that it is supernatural. It is not just wishful thought or some kind sentiment. It is something that is supernaturally empowered and determines people's destiny. This is true of blessings and curses alike.

One whole chapter of Deuteronomy 28 is devoted

to showing the various forms that blessings and curses can take. The first fourteen verses deal with blessings and the remaining fifty four verses deal with curses. In verses 1 and 2 Moses deals first with the cause of blessings: "If you diligently obey the voice of the Lord your God, to observe carefully all His commandments ... all these blessings shall come upon you and overtake you, because you obey the voice of the Lord your God."

Under the new covenant, in John 10:27, Jesus similarly described those whom He acknowledged as "His sheep"—that is His true disciples: "My sheep hear My voice... and they follow Me." The basic requirements are still the same: hearing the Lord's voice and following Him in obedience.

"It is something that is supernaturally empowered and determines people's destiny."

The cause of curses is exactly the opposite to that of blessings. Curses result from not hearing God's voice and not doing what He says. This refusal to hear and obey God's voice can be summed up in one word: rebellion — not against man, but against God.

Out of my own studies, I have attempted to make two lists that sum up the blessings and the curses in the order in which they are mentioned in Deuteronomy 28. My suggested list of blessings is as follows:

- Exaltation
- Health
- Reproductiveness
- Prosperity
- Victory
- God's favour

In the list of curses, Moses goes into much greater detail than with the blessings. Essentially, however, the curses are the opposite of the blessings. Here is my suggested summary:

- Humiliation
- Barrenness, unfruitfulness
- Mental and physical sickness
- Family breakdown
- Poverty
- Defeat, failure
- Oppression
- God's disfavour

In verse 13, Moses concludes his list of blessings with a vivid verbal picture. Each of us would do well to consider how this picture might apply in our own lives.

He says: "The Lord will make you the head and not the tail..." I once asked the Lord to show me how this would apply in my life. I felt He gave me this answer: the head makes the decisions and the tail just gets dragged around.

Are you acting like a head, in control of each situation, making the appropriate decisions and seeing them successfully carried out? Or are you merely playing the part of the tail, being dragged around by forces and circumstances you don't understand and cannot control?

PART 2
The Source of Curses

Solomon makes it clear in Proverbs 26:2 that there is always a reason for every curse.

Like a flitting sparrow, like a flying swallow,
So a curse without cause shall not alight.

This principle has a double application. On one hand, a curse cannot take effect unless there is a cause for it. On the other hand, the opposite is also true. Wherever there is a curse at work, there is a cause for it. We need discernment from the Holy Spirit not only to pinpoint the cause of curses but also the source of curses. If you can discover the cause of your particular problem you will be in a much better position to deal with it effectively.

This section opens up the causes of the main curses that commonly afflict our lives. After reading it you will be better able to understand and apply God's remedy, which is unfolded in the following section.

03 | God as a Source of Curses

Many people are hindered by a defective understanding of the character of God. They think they see the Old Testament showing God as a God of wrath and judgment and in the New Testament as a God of love and mercy.

However both parts of the Scripture are consistent with each other and we need both to have an accurate picture of God. In Romans 11:22 Paul presents these two aspects of God's dealings side by side: *"Therefore consider the goodness* [or kindness] *and severity of God."* His blessings arise from His kindness, but His judgments proceed out of His severity. Both are equally real.

Many times God has pronounced a curse on individuals or even on whole nations. His purpose is to get people's attention, warning them of the terrible consequences of disobedience. A curse is one of God's severest forms of judgment but His desire is always for people to repent and turn back to Him.

One of the earliest examples of God being the source of a curse is found in the call of Abraham in Genesis 12. There were actually seven stages to this call and six of them are promises of God's blessing but there is also a solemn warning:

(1) I will make you a great nation

(2) I will bless you

(3) And make your name great

(4) And you shall be a blessing

(5) I will bless those who bless you,

(6) And I will curse him who curses you;

(7) And in you all the families of the earth will be blessed.

Genesis 12:1-3

Notice that the sixth part of God's call to Abram is a curse on everyone who curses Abram. That goes for Abram and his descendants. When God calls a man to a special task, that man becomes a particular target for the opposition of Satan so God builds in a protective clause for him.

Later on in Genesis 27:29 when Isaac blessed his

son Jacob, he extended the same protection, "Cursed be everyone who curses you." Thus both the blessing and curse that God originally pronounced on Abraham were also extended to his descendants. It is vital to see that this directly extends to the Jewish people as a whole and the nation of Israel.

Notice that God did not make it impossible for His enemies to curse or persecute Abraham and his descendants but He did ensure that there would be terrible consequences for doing so. The whole tragic history of anti-Semitism bears sobering witness to this. Anti-Semitism brings a curse from God.

"A curse is one of God's severest forms of judgment but His desire is always for people to repent and turn back to Him."

Unfortunately, throughout many centuries, the professing Christian church has often been guilty of spreading shameful anti-Semitism. Yet the Church owes every spiritual blessing she claims to those who have been her victims: the Jewish people. Without the Jews, the Church would have had no apostles, no Bible and no Saviour.

Maybe you or your ancestors have been enemies of the Jewish people. You may have criticized them or cursed them. Such actions have consequences; it will bring a curse on your life. However, you can be set free.

Disobedience

In Deuteronomy 27:11-26 God ordained that when Israel came into their promised land, they were to pronounce upon themselves twelve curses if they disobeyed God in certain respects. They couldn't enter into the promised land without being exposed to both a blessing if they were obedient and a curse if they were disobedient. Between these two there was no middle ground. No other option was open to them.

Twelve specific and detailed curses were listed which could be summarized under the following headings:

- idolatry and worshipping false gods
- dishonouring parents
- illicit or unnatural sex
- injustice toward the weak and helpless

Idolatry and Worshipping False Gods

In Exodus 20:3, the first of the Ten Commandments, the Lord said, "I am the Lord your God...you shall have no other gods besides me...you shall make no graven image to worship." So we see that worshipping false gods and all forms of idolatry are direct disobedience to God. The true God, revealed first in creation and then more fully in Scripture, is holy, awesome, glorious, omnipotent. To represent Him in the likeness of any created being — whether human or animal — is to offer Him a deliberate insult. No wonder it provokes God's wrath.

> *Cursed is the one who makes a carved or moulded image, an abomination to the Lord, the work of the hands of the craftsman, and sets it up in secret.*
>
> *Deuteronomy 27:15*

However, there is also a second, wider range of practices that are not necessarily openly idolatrous, or even religious. Because their true nature is concealed by deceptive terminology, they are appropriately described as occult (derived from a Latin word meaning "hidden" or "covered over").

These occult practices focus on two of the strongest cravings of human nature which are the desire for knowledge and the desire for power. Up to a certain point, man is able to satisfy these cravings from natural sources and by natural means. If he is not fully satisfied by what he obtains in this way, he will inevitably turn to supernatural sources. It is at this point that he easily becomes entrapped in the occult.

The reason for this is that there are actually only two available sources of supernatural knowledge and power in the universe: either God or Satan. If such supernatural knowledge and power is derived from God, it is legitimate; if derived from Satan it is illegitimate. It was this craving for illegitimate knowledge from the forbidden tree of the knowledge of good and evil that motivated man's first transgression in the Garden of Eden. By doing so, man crossed an invisible boundary into Satan's territory. Ever since then man has been vulnerable to deception.

"...there are only two available sources of supernatural knowledge and power in the universe: either God or Satan.

The variety of forms of deception that such illegitimate, occult practices can take is virtually unlimited. However, it is possible to identify three main branches: witchcraft, sorcery and divination.

Witchcraft is the *power* branch of the occult. Its root is exposed by a brief statement in 1 Samuel 15:23: "For rebellion is as the sin of witchcraft." Witchcraft is an expression of man's rebellion against God. It is man's attempt to gain his own ends without submitting to God's law. Its driving force is a desire to control people and circumstances. To gain this end it may use either psychological pressures or psychic techniques, or a combination of both to manipulate, intimidate and dominate.

Divination is the *knowledge* branch of the occult, offering many different forms of knowledge that cannot be obtained by purely natural means. In its commonest form, as *fortune-telling*, it offers supernatural knowledge of the future. It also includes all false forms of religious revelation that claim a supernatural source.

Sorcery operates through *material objects* or through other ways of impacting the physical senses, such as *drugs* and *music*. In Revelation 9:21 the word for sorceries is directly derived from the Greek word for *drugs*. Many different kinds of physical objects can be used: religious artefacts, pagan fetishes or charms, amulets, ouija boards are just some of the more common examples. It is important to recognize that books can be channels of occult power. Christians in Ephesus (Acts 19:18,19) recognized that their many occult scrolls were a source of bondage so, despite their considerable value, they gathered them and burned them. The only appropriate way to deal with such occult materials is to destroy them completely.

Those who trespass in these occult areas are seeking from Satan the supernatural knowledge or power that God does not permit man to seek from any other source but Himself. In so doing, they are, in fact, acknowledging Satan as a god besides the one true God, and are thus breaking the first of the Ten Commandments.

In this way they are exposing themselves to the curse God has pronounced on all who break His commandments — a curse that extends as far as the fourth generation. All Israel had to invoke upon themselves a curse if they became involved in idolatry, in worshipping false gods or in what we call these days, the occult, in all its various forms.

This is the primary cause of curses in people's lives. God says that if we do get involved in such practices, *"I will require it of the three following generations. It will not only be visited on you but for three subsequent generations."*

So you may be struggling with something in your life right now which is caused by your parents, your grandparents or even your great-grandparents or some other ancestor. You see how important it is to diagnose and identify the problem so that it can be effectively dealt with.

Thank God He has provided a way of release from any curse that might have come from this source! His provision is available for us. In the final day of reckoning, God will not hold against us the fact that our ancestors brought a curse upon us, but He will hold us guilty if we refuse to receive the provision He has made for us to be released from such a curse.

Dishonouring Parents

We have to be very careful at this point. While it may be true that some of our problems can be traced back to the actions of others, we must beware of blaming others for things that we alone are responsible for.

Particular care is needed as we view our relationship with our parents. Countless people today — including many Christians — are unaware that disrespect for parents brings God's curse. Many people have problems in their lives because their attitude to their parents is not right. Even though no parent is perfect, this does not mean they do not deserve respect as parents. Remember that the first commandment with a blessing is expressed in a positive way, "Honour your father and your mother that your days may be long upon the land which the Lord your God is giving you."

Throughout my whole ministry, I have never met a person who dishonoured their parents and had life go well for them. Never. Such behaviour automatically exposes you to a curse. I don't mean you have to agree with your parents or even do everything they tell you to do — that depends on the way your parents are living — but you have to honour them as your parents. I have met so many whose lives have been straightened out when they put right their attitude toward their parents.

I think of others who never did it and who never were blessed. I think of one member of my family who died of cancer at the age of forty. He was saved, baptized in the Holy Spirit and served the Lord, but he never enjoyed the blessing of God because he never put right his relationship with his mother. She was a spiritist, so she had all the problems you can imagine. He could have escaped from these problems if he had dealt with his relationship with his mother. I am not teaching about theories — I am teaching about things I know from experience.

"Many people have problems in their lives because their attitude to their parents is not right."

Illicit or Unnatural Sex

Any form of unnatural sex brings a curse. This includes any form of homosexuality or bestiality. Sexual relationships with members of your family outside the permitted range will also bring a curse. Sadly, today we have to acknowledge that there are millions of children who are victimized by their fathers in the area of sex.

Injustice Toward the Weak and Helpless

Because the American government regularly broke its treaties with the various American Indian tribes, the Indians placed a curse on the White House.

That is why, from 1860 until 1980, every President elected in the 20th year died in office. You can trace that back to two things. The American government's unfaithfulness to the American Indians and the fact that Abraham Lincoln, who was the President elected in 1860, permitted a spiritist seance to be conducted in the White House by his wife. She later died in a mental institute. See how involvement in such activity doesn't just affect individuals, it can also affect whole nations.

I believe President Reagan would also have died in office — as you know, an attempt was made on his life early in his presidency. However, just before he took the oath as President, a group of us in a large meeting, combined in prayer and faith and released not just him but also the presidency from the curse. You see how close the curse came to being fulfilled; the bullet lodged within an inch of his heart. I believe that was God's vindication of the prayer that released the curse. This is no abstract theory; such things negatively affect the lives of people and nations everywhere.

Self Reliance

A completely different kind of curse is found in

Jeremiah 17:5,6.

> *Thus says the Lord:*
> *"Cursed is the man who trusts in man*
> *And makes flesh his strength*
> *Whose heart departs from the Lord*

[and this is the curse]

> *For he shall be like a shrub in the desert,*
> *And shall not see when good comes,*
> *But shall inhabit the parched places*
> *in the wilderness,*
> *In a salt land which is not inhabited.*

This is typical of a person living under a curse. Everybody else is receiving the rain (the blessing, the prosperity) but in the midst of it all, he lives in a parched land and never experiences the blessing for himself. Why? Because of the curse. Cursed is the man who relies on human ability and material resources and whose heart departs from the Lord. This does not necessarily show a desire to do evil but it is evidence of a desire to be independent of God. Such people may even seek to perform righteous acts but without depending on the supernatural grace of God.

I believe that this curse rests on many Christian churches which have tasted of the grace of God but then turned away and began trusting in their own efforts, intelligence and religion. Like the Galatians, they may have "begun in the Spirit" but they have ended up operating in the flesh. The blessing of God has lifted and a curse has come upon them. I have preached in many churches that I was assured were under a curse. No matter how you preach, fight and struggle there are very few results until the curse is dealt with.

"Cursed is the man who relies on human ability and material resources and whose heart departs from the Lord."

Theft and Perjury

The last three prophets of the Old Testament, Haggai, Zechariah and Malachi, all deal with various areas in which Israel experienced the outworking of God's curse. In Zechariah 5:1-4, the prophet had a vision of a scroll that contained curses on both sides. One side was on the person who stole; the other was on the person who perjured and swore falsely in the name of the Lord.

A vivid picture follows of the destruction that comes in the outworking of this curse. In biblical Hebrew, the word "house" applies not just to the material structure, but to the people who live in it. The widespread breakdown of family life we see today is just one sign of the ultimate effect of such a curse. Without repentance and restitution it could lead to the erosion of whole nations and even an entire civilization. I wonder how many people today would be under a curse if you included all those who stole and perjured themselves. How many are not honest in their tax returns? In every country this would include many people; how many of them would be church goers?

Haggai 1:4-6 paints a similar picture of people sowing much yet harvesting little and putting their wages into a bag full of holes. God had to send Israel a prophet to show them that the invisible force eroding their provisions was a curse that they had brought on themselves by putting their own selfish concerns before the needs of God's house.

04 | Curses From Authority Figures

As we have seen, both blessings and curses are part of a vast, invisible spiritual realm, which affects each of our lives. One central and decisive factor in this realm is authority. Without an understanding of the principles of authority, it is impossible to function effectively in the realm of the spirit.

Men Representing God

Throughout the universe there is one and only one, supreme source of authority: God the Creator. God does not normally exercise His authority directly, however, but delegates it to others of His choice. The authority that such a person exercises on behalf of God includes, among other things, the ability to bless and to curse.

Even though we have seen in this century a worldwide revolt against authority, the principle of authority still operates just as surely as the principle of gravity.

A few examples of men representing God will be enough to demonstrate the principle. In Joshua 6:26, when the children of Israel miraculously captured the city of Jericho, Joshua pronounced a curse on anyone who would rebuild it. That was about 1300 BC. About five hundred years later, as we read in 1 Kings 16:34, a man named Hiel from Bethel attempted to rebuild on the same site. It cost him the lives of two of his children. For no apparent medical reason they just wasted away. No doctor could diagnose it yet here was the direct outworking of the curse pronounced by Joshua. In your own life you may be dealing with things caused by something that goes back hundreds of years.

Another example is found in David's words in his song after the death of Saul and Jonathan in 2 Samuel 1:21. David was a tremendous curser — I don't mean in the sense that many use that word today. He pronounced some horrific curses on some people; yet this is part of the ministry of a man of God.

This is what he said in this beautiful song about Saul and Jonathan:

O mountains of Gilboa;

Let there be no dew, nor let there be
rain upon you,
Nor fields of offerings.
For the shield of the mighty is cast
away there!
The shield of Saul not anointed with oil.

Even though these words were spoken more than 3000 years ago, you can go to the mountains of Gilboa today and there is still no green vegetation on them. Despite the diligent efforts of the government of Israel to replant forest, nothing would grow there! All because of words spoken by David 3000 years ago.

Remember Gehazi who was the servant of the prophet Elisha? Gehazi disobeyed Elisha and ran off to Naaman who had just been miraculously healed. He asked for money and clothing and hid these from Elisha. When he came back Elisha said, "Didn't my spirit go with you?" Then he said this, "Therefore the leprosy of Naaman shall cling to you and your descendants forever." And he went out from his presence leprous as white as snow (2 Kings 5:27). What was that the result of? A curse spoken by a man of God.

People With Relational Authority

This is another source of curses which is very important. God has so ordered human society that in certain situations one person has authority over another person or people.

The most obvious example is a father, who, according to the Word of God, has authority over his family. Whether people like it or not, whether they fight it or not, is unimportant — the fact is, he has authority over his family. If he doesn't use it that is his problem.

Another person who has authority is the husband over his wife. They are very closely related. The Bible says God is the head of Christ, Christ is the head of the husband and the husband is the head of the woman. Feminists can say what they like about it, but the fact remains that it is true. You can't change the reality of it by objecting to it.

Look at the case of Jacob and his family. Jacob had served his uncle, Laban, for more than fourteen years. He had acquired two wives, and concubines and eleven children. Then he decided to flee back to the land that God had promised him. Jacob fled secretly because he was afraid that Laban would claim his wives back — they were Laban's daughters after all.

When they fled, Rachel, who was Jacob's second wife, stole her father's household gods. He shouldn't have had household gods and she shouldn't have stolen them but she did. This made Laban very angry so he pursued them and when he caught up with them, he accused Jacob of stealing his gods.

Jacob was unaware of what Rachel had done so he was indignant at being accused. In Genesis 31:32 he said, "With whomever you find your gods, do not let him live." This is actually a curse, unwittingly pronounced by Jacob over his own wife.

Tragically they were not empty words but were charged with his relational authority. He actually spoke into being the destiny of his wife; the next time she had a child, she died in childbirth. What a sobering situation.

"You would be amazed at how many people struggle all through their lives because of a parental curse..."

Fathers also exercise a role that has similar influence. Second to the blessing of God, the most desirable thing in life is a father's blessing. And one of the things to be feared most is a father's curse. Many fathers have put a curse on their children without knowing it. I know this because I have dealt with so many and helped them out of it.

Imagine a father with three children. The first and the third are clever but the middle one is not so bright and the father doesn't like this one as much. (I have noticed this about parents — if there is one of their children they don't like; it is usually the one most like themselves. I think they don't like what they fear in themselves.) The father may say to this child, "You'll never succeed. Your brothers are good but you'll be a failure all your life."

Do you know what that is? A curse. Of course it is equally possible for a mother to say such equally damaging things either about or to her children. You would be amazed at how many people struggle all through their lives because of a parental curse like this pronounced over them.

Beyond the Family

Teachers are another kind of person who can pronounce curses because of the authority they have over children. It may be that a teacher in the early years has one pupil that she really can't get on with. She may say things like, "You'll never learn. You just haven't got it; you'll never succeed." Once again I have had to deal with people who needed to be delivered of such a curse spoken by a teacher.

Because of the spiritual authority he has over his congregation, a pastor is another person who has the power to speak either positive or negative things over the lives of their people. Suppose a pastor has a clash with a member of his congregation, and that person leaves, maybe in a bad spirit. The pastor may say, "Wherever you go, you'll never succeed until you put things right with this church."

Once again this is a curse. Religious groups are often terrible in this way; if you break away from some groups they will automatically put a curse on you. Believe me, this is not something which is of no consequence; it is very real.

Servants of Satan

Attitudes toward Satan among Christians vary between two extremes. Some ignore Satan totally and try to act as if he is not real. Others are afraid of him and give him far more attention than he deserves. Between these extremes is a proper scriptural balance.

The name Satan means "adversary" or "opposer". He is the unchanging, determined enemy of God Himself and of the people and purposes of God. His goal is to bring the whole human race under his control. His primary tactic is deception, of which he is a master.

Satan already exercises dominion over the great majority of mankind — all those who are in an attitude of rebellion against God. In Ephesians 2:2 he is described as "the spirit who now works in the sons of disobedience." Most of these have no clear picture of their real condition. They are simply driven to and fro by forces they do not understand and cannot control.

"His primary tactic is deception, of which he is a master."

There are those among them, however, who have deliberately opened themselves up to Satan, even though they may not be aware of his true identity. In pursuit of power and material gain they systematically cultivate the exercise of the supernatural forces Satan has released to them. Such servants of Satan are recognized in almost every culture and have been given a variety of titles. Witchdoctor, medicine man and shaman are perhaps the most widely used but each culture has its own terms.

Jesus did not deny that Satan was real or that he had power. But He promised His disciples that the authority He gave them would make them victorious over Satan's power and would protect them against all his attempts to harm them.

Curses are one of the main weapons that servants of Satan use against the people of God. This is vividly illustrated by the story of Balak and Balaam in Numbers 22-24. The king of Moab knew he couldn't defeat Israel in war so he hired Balaam and asked him to pronounce a curse on them. Even today, if tribes fight each other, the witchdoctor will put a curse on their enemies before they go into battle.

However, each time Balaam tried to curse Israel, God intervened and turned the proposed curses into blessings! It is important to realize that God did not view Balaam's proposed curse against Israel as just empty words that had no power. He regarded them as a serious threat to Israel and this is why He intervened personally to frustrate Balaam's intention. Time has not changed God's viewpoint. He does not ignore or belittle curses directed against His people by servants of Satan. On the contrary, He equips His people with superior power.

When God's people avail themselves of that power and the grip of curses is broken, the difference in people's lives is amazing. Many areas of the world are dominated by the unseen spiritual power of witchdoctors. In Africa we have seen dramatic changes in people's lives after they have been released from curses by confession and prayer. People who before, would hardly smile, became some of the happiest people. The change was like from night to day.

On one occasion, one particular man came up to us after a meeting. He was well-dressed yet he rubbed himself in the dust, which was their way of showing appreciation. He said, "I've been a wretched man all my life. I've been in continual pain for years. Now I am free. I have no more pain and I am happy."

The only thing that had happened was that we had released him from the curse. We have become so civilized in some places that we have lost touch with some things that are very real. Even if we don't believe in them we can still be affected by them.

05 | Self-Imposed Curses and Soulish Talk

We have seen that words, whether spoken or written, can have mighty effect for both good or evil. We have all experienced times when words have been a source of encouragement that give us hope to go on. They may be words that others have spoken to us or we may have spoken them to ourselves. Unfortunately, many people do not realize that it is also very possible, by their own words, to have a strongly negative impact upon themselves and others. By doing this they are actually pronouncing curses upon themselves.

Self-Imposed Curses

Think again of the story of Rebekah and Jacob. Remember that Rebekah had persuaded Jacob to get the blessing of his father Isaac ahead of his older brother Esau, to whom it rightfully belonged. Jacob was smart and thought ahead of what could happen and so in Genesis 27:12, 13 he said,

> *"Perhaps my father will feel me and I
> shall seem to be a deceiver to him; and I
> shall bring a curse upon myself and not a
> blessing." But his mother said to him, "Let
> your curse be upon me, my son."*

In so doing she pronounced the curse on herself. Later on in the chapter she complained to her husband Isaac about the wives that Esau had married and she didn't approve of. Rebekah wasn't getting things the way she wanted them so she said to Isaac,

> *"I am weary of my life because of the
> daughters of Heth; if Jacob takes a wife of
> the children of Heth, like those who are the
> daughters of the land, what good will my life
> be to me?"*

> *Genesis 27:46*

She had pronounced a double curse on herself. She said she was weary of her life and asked what the good was of living — she felt she might as well die.

I cannot tell you how many people we have dealt with who have pronounced such a curse on themselves by saying, "I wish I were dead. What's the use of living? I'm not going to make it." You don't have to say something like that very often. This is like an open invitation to the spirit of death and you don't have to give many invitations; he will come in. We have seen scores of people delivered from the spirit of death.

At one meeting in Northern Ireland, I prayed collectively for the people that needed deliverance from the spirit of death. In an audience of about 2000 people about 50 people, most of them young, received simultaneous deliverance!

"...there was one kind of curse from which even God could not protect His people: the curse they pronounced on themselves."

How does this attitude of hopelessness come in? By saying things like, "It's no good living. What's life got to offer me? I might as well be dead." These are terribly dangerous things to say because you are really pronouncing a curse on yourself. You may say

"But I didn't really mean it" but Jesus has a solemn warning against careless, idle words like this. In Matthew 12:36,37 He said,

> *"But I say to you that for every idle word*
> *men may speak, they will give account of it*
> *in the day of judgment.*
> *For by your words you will be*
> *justified and by your words you will*
> *be condemned."*

The fact that the speaker "doesn't really mean them" does not in any way minimize or cancel the effect of his words. Nor does it release him from his accountability. How much the devil would like to trick you into saying things like that. Often such things are said for very inadequate reasons. You may be upset or discouraged and say something like that without realizing its significance yet you could well be settling your own destiny.

A more tragic and far-reaching example of a self-imposed curse is found in Matthew 27:24, 25. The scene is the trial of Jesus by Pontius Pilate.

> *When Pilate saw that he could not prevail*

> *at all, but rather that a tumult was rising,*
> *he took water and washed his hands*
> *before the multitude, saying,*
> *"I am innocent of the blood of this just*
> *person. You see to it."*
> *And all the people answered and said,*
> *"His blood be upon us and upon our*
> *children."*

You really cannot understand the history of the Jewish people over the last nineteen centuries until you see that one major factor in it is this self-imposed curse which goes on from generation to generation. Only God knows how much persecution and suffering of the Jews can be traced back to this source. Earlier we saw how God provided protection for Jacob and his descendants — the Jewish people — from all who would seek to put a curse on them. However there was one kind of curse from which even God could not protect His people: *the curse they pronounced on themselves.*

Unscriptural Covenants

In Exodus 23:32, as they were about to enter the promised land, God warned Israel against the wicked, idolatrous nations that were there, "You shall make no covenant with them, nor with their gods."

A covenant is the most solemn and powerful form of relationship into which a person can enter. Satan is well aware of this and he therefore exploits covenant relationships of his own making in order to gain the strongest possible control over people. If you make a covenant with people who are under the power of evil forces, then you come under the influence of that same power.

This is particularly true of secret societies. The Freemasons are the clearest example of this on a worldwide scale. In order to be initiated, a person has to bind himself by the most cruel and barbarous oaths never to reveal any of Masonry's secrets. It would be impossible to find anywhere a more frightening example of self-imposed curses than these oaths.

Masonry is a *false religion* because it acknowledges a false god. Many of the objects and symbols associated with Christianity — including the Bible

— are used in Masonry, but this is a deliberate deception. The god whom Masonry acknowledges is *not* the God of the Bible.

Any involvement with such groups is a sure road to disaster for you and your descendants. Only God knows the number of crippled, retarded, unhappy children whose problems originate from a parent's involvement with the Freemasons. You can do what you like about it, but the consequences are ordered by God and you can't change them.

> *"Covenants of all sorts are powerful and binding."*

Covenants of all sorts are powerful and binding. You are not free to make a covenant with people on the basis of anything but the covenant that is made in the blood of Jesus.

It should be clear by now that our words can have a powerful impact, which can be either positive or negative in its effect. Talk or even prayer that originates from a person's soul produces negative results in a similar manner to self-imposed curses. Many Christians may be surprised at this but it is important to realize that James is writing both to and about Christians when he warns:

> *But if you have bitter envy and self-*
> *seeking in your hearts, do not boast and*
> *lie against the truth. For this wisdom does*
> *not descend from above, but is earthly,*
> *sensual, demonic.*
>
> James 3:14-15

The key to understanding the downward process lies in the word 'sensual'. The Greek word is *psuchikos*, formed directly from *psuche*, meaning 'soul'. The corresponding English word would be 'soulish'.

In 1 Thesssalonians 5:23 Paul prays, "Now may the God of peace Himself sanctify you completely; and may your whole spirit, soul and body be preserved blameless." Paul here puts together the three elements that make up a complete human personality, listing them in descending order from the highest to the lowest: first spirit, then soul, then body.

At the fall, as a result of man's disobedience, his spirit was cut off from God. At the same time his soul began to express itself independently of his spirit. This new, 'disjointed' relationship was both the consequence and the expression of man's rebellion against God.

1 Corinthians 2:14-15 and Jude 16-17 help us understand what a natural or soulish person is like. While the spiritual person is functioning according to God's will, the soulish person is out of harmony with God. He may associate with the church and even appear to be a Christian but in reality his rebellious attitude and conduct grieve the Spirit of God and cause offence in the Body of Christ.

This can be manifested through the words a person says in a number of ways. In Romans 1:29-30 Paul lists some of the consequences of man's turning away from God. Here is part of the list, "They are full of envy, murder, strife, deceit and malice. They are gossips, slanderers, God-haters, insolent, arrogant and boastful" (NIV). The inclusion of gossip in such a list shows how seriously God considers this sin.

In a similar way James warns us, "Do not speak evil of one another, brethren" (James 4:11). The original Greek means "to speak against", so we are not to speak against fellow-believers — even if what we say about them is true. This does not rule out speaking the truth to one another (notice the preposition), as long as we go to the person involved first (following

Matthew 18:15-17), and in an attitude of love and humility (according to Ephesians 4:15).

This same humility and purity of motive will cause us to rely on the Holy Spirit's help in prayer so that we know not only *what* to pray for but *how* to pray for it. We are totally dependent on the Holy Spirit's help to pray effectively. In Romans 8:26-27 Paul puts it very clearly:

> *Likewise the Spirit also helps our weak-nesses. For we do not know what we should pray for as we ought, but the Spirit Himself makes intercession for us with groanings that cannot be uttered. Now He who searches the hearts knows what the mind of the Spirit is, because He makes intercession for the saints according to the will of God.*

There is much that could be said about such prayer but here I just want to make the point that while many people assume that prayer is always acceptable to God and its effects are always good, this is not the case.

If we do not submit ourselves to the Holy Spirit and seek His direction, then our prayers may well be motivated by fleshly attitudes such as envy, self-seeking, resentment, anger or criticism. The Holy Spirit will not endorse prayers that proceed from such attitudes, nor will He present them before God the Father.

Inevitably therefore, our praying degenerates into the pattern we have seen in James 3:15: earthly — soulish — demonic. The effect of such soulish prayers is like that of soulish talk; negative not positive. It releases against those for whom we are praying invisible, indefinable pressures, which do not relieve their burdens, but rather add to them.

"There are some people who pray for you whose prayers you would be better off without."

There are some people who pray for you whose prayers you would be better off without. That may sound shocking, but some people have their own ideas what other people's ministry should be, where they should go and so on. They may try to pray that into being but it may not be the will of God at all. You may experience pressure against you every time you try to do certain things that they are praying against.

There is hardly such a thing as prayer that is not effective. The question is not whether our prayers are effective. The question is whether their effect is positive or negative. That is determined by the power that works through them. Are they really from the Holy Spirit? Or are they a soulish counterfeit? The power of soulish prayer is both real and dangerous. The result it produces is not a blessing, but a curse.

06 | Seven Indications of a Curse

Through personal observation and experience I have compiled the following list of seven problem areas indicating that a curse is at work. The presence of only one or two of these problems would not necessarily be sufficient, by itself, to establish conclusively the working of a curse. But when several of the problems are present, or when any one of them tends to occur repeatedly, the probability of a curse increases proportionately. In the last resort, however, we need the Holy Spirit's discernment for it is only He who can provide an absolutely accurate "diagnosis".

1. Mental and/or emotional breakdown

If a breakdown happens just once in a life, there could be other causes. However, if it is a thing that recurs frequently in a family, you can be sure that the family is under a curse. Confusion and depression are often associated and these almost invariably have their roots in some form of occult involvement and/or demonic activity.

2. Repeated or chronic illness

This does not necessarily indicate that every form of sickness is a direct result of a curse. It is particularly significant when there is no clear medical diagnosis. If certain types of sickness are hereditary, in other words, passed down from generation to generation, this is also a common sign of the effect of a curse.

3. Barrenness, a tendency to miscarry or related female problems

Quite often problems connected with the reproductive process can affect all the females in a family. If women come for prayer for such problems, which Ruth and I pray for frequently, we instruct them on the nature and causes of curses and then pray with them for release. We have seen many dramatically changed.

4. Breakdown of marriage and family alienation

Malachi 4:5-6 paints a grim picture of

conditions in the world just before this age closes. The prophet shows an evil force at work, alienating parents from children and producing a breakdown of family relationships. Unless God intervenes, he warns, this curse that is destroying family life will be extended to the whole earth.

5. Continuing financial insufficiency

Deuteronomy 28:47-48 presents a graphic picture of the outworking of a curse:

> *Because you did not serve the Lord your God joyfully and gladly in the time of prosperity, therefore in hunger and thirst, in nakedness and dire poverty, you will serve the enemies the Lord sends against you.*
>
> *(NIV)*

Taken together, these two verses point to a simple conclusion: prosperity is a blessing and poverty is a curse. God's will for His people is abundance, as Paul summed it up in 2 Corinthians 9:8,

And God is able to make all grace abound

> *toward you, that you, always having*
> *all sufficiency in all things, have an*
> *abundance for every good work.*

Poverty is having less than you need to do all God's will for your life. Abundance, on the other hand, is having all you need to do God's will — and something over to give to others.

6. Being "accident-prone"

Some people have an unusual number of strange accidents. It almost seems that there is an unseen, malicious force working against such people. It is a condition that can be identified by statistical analysis. Some insurance companies raise the premiums of people considered unusually high risks.

7. A history of suicides and unnatural or untimely deaths

A curse that takes this form often affects not just a single individual but a larger social unit such as a family or tribe. Normally, too, it continues from one generation to the next.

The above list of seven indications of a curse is by

no means exhaustive. Others could be added. You have probably read far enough by now, however, to take stock of your situation.

PART 3
How to Be Set Free

Have you come to see by now that your life may somehow have been blighted by a curse? Are you wondering if there is a way out from under the dark shadow that has been shutting out the sunlight of God's blessing? You do not have to be dominated by the effects of curses; whether they originate during your lifetime or as a result of the actions of previous generations. You can know freedom from pressures you thought you had to live with.

Very often we need to ascertain the cause or the source of the curse — not always, but very often. That is why I have outlined in previous sections the various possibilities, because I am trusting the Holy Spirit to speak to you as you read. I am not saying you have to know, but in many cases God wants us to know what we are being delivered from, and how it came upon us. If God shows you, then act on what He shows you.

Yes, there is a way out! But there is only one: through the sacrificial death of Jesus on the cross. This section will explain in simple, practical terms how you may find and follow God's way — from shadow to sunlight, from curse to blessing.

07 | The Divine Exchange

The entire message of the Gospel revolves around one unique historical event: the sacrificial death of Jesus on the cross. Concerning this the writer of Hebrews says: *"For by one offering* [**sacrifice**] *He* [**Jesus**] *has perfected forever those who are being sanctified"* **(Hebrews 10:14). Two powerful expressions are combined:** *"perfected"* **and** *"forever"*. **Together, they depict a sacrifice that comprehends every need of the entire human race. Furthermore, its effects extend throughout time and on into eternity.**

This is the essential foundation to our release. At the cross a divinely ordained exchange took place. First, Jesus endured in our place all the evil consequences that we deserved because of our sin. In exchange, God offers us all the good that was due to the sinless obedience of Jesus.

Let us briefly summarize all that was accomplished on the cross so that you have an appreciation of the scope of redemption.

Jesus was punished that we might be forgiven.
Jesus was wounded that we might be healed.

These two truths are interwoven. In the spiritual dimension Jesus received the punishment due to our sin that we, in turn, might be forgiven and have peace with God.

In the physical dimension, Jesus took our sicknesses and pains so that we, through His wounds, might be healed.

Jesus was made sin with our sinfulness that we
might become righteous with His righteousness.

A third aspect of the exchange is revealed in Isaiah 53:10, which states that the Lord made the soul of Jesus "an offering for sin." All of this was foreshadowed in the regulations given to Moses for the various forms of sin offering.

In 2 Corinthians 5:21 Paul refers to Isaiah 53:10 and at the same time he also presents the positive aspect of the exchange: "For He [God] made Him[Jesus] who knew no sin to be sin for us, that we might become the righteousness of God in Him." We can never earn this righteousness, it can only be received by faith.

Jesus died our death
that we might share His life.

The entire Bible emphasizes that the final outcome of sin is death. When Jesus became identified with our sin, it was inevitable that He should also experience the death that is the outcome of human sin.

In return, to all who accept His substitutionary sacrifice, He now offers the gift of eternal life. In Romans 6:23 Paul sets the two alternatives side by side: "For the wages [just reward] of sin is death, but the [unearned] gift of God is eternal life in Christ Jesus our Lord."

Jesus became poor with our poverty
that we might become rich with His riches.

In Deuteronomy 28:48 Moses summed up absolute poverty in four expressions: hunger, thirst, nakedness and need of all things. Jesus experienced all this on the cross so that we might experience His abundance.

Very often our "abundance" will be like that of Jesus while He was on earth. We shall not carry large sums of cash, or have large deposits in a bank. But from day to day we shall have enough for our own needs and something over for the needs of others.

Jesus bore our shame that we might share His glory.

He endured our rejection that we might have His acceptance as children of God.

The exchange at the cross covers also the emotional forms of suffering that follow from man's iniquity. Two of the cruelest wounds brought upon us by our iniquity are shame and rejection. Execution on a cross was the most shameful and degrading of all forms of death. On the cross Jesus also endured the agonizing rejection of a broken relationship with the Father. When He called out to the Father there was no response. Once again, Jesus endured the evil that we in turn might enjoy the good.

Jesus became a curse
that we might receive the blessing.

Paul sums up this aspect of the exchange in Galatians 3:13-14:

> *Christ has redeemed us from the curse*
> *of the law, having become a curse for us*
> *(for it is written, "Cursed is everyone who*
> *hangs on a tree"),*
> *that the blessing of Abraham might come*
> *upon the Gentiles in Christ Jesus, that*
> *we might receive the promise of the Spirit*
> *through faith.*

This is the basis of our deliverance. It has to be based on faith in what Christ has done for us on the cross. Just as we are made righteous because He was made sinful, so we can receive the blessing because He was made the curse. The Law of Moses says in Deuteronomy 21:23, anyone hung on a tree becomes a curse. Every Jew who knew the Law of Moses, when they saw Jesus hanging on the cross, knew that

He had been made a curse. Thank God, the reason He was made a curse was that we might be delivered from the curse.

You need to bear in mind that after you have been delivered you still have to go on meeting the conditions, which are listening to God's voice and doing what He says. In John 10:27 Jesus said, "My sheep hear my voice, and I know them and they follow me."

So that is the prescription for blessing, but in order to live in blessing, if there is a curse over your life, you must first be redeemed from the curse — be delivered. Through the death of Jesus it is already legally ours. He has obtained it for us. What we have to do is move from the legal to the experiential; we have to get it working in our lives. I want to tell you how to do that. The legal base is already there. God doesn't have to do any more, we have to appropriate what God has done for us.

08 | Seven Steps to Release

Salvation is a word that sums up the total work that God desires to do in our lives. In some ways the scope of this work is obscured by the various ways the original Greek verb *sozo* is translated in different parts of the New Testament. It is normally translated "to save" but is also used in a variety of ways that go beyond the forgiveness of sins.

It is used, for instance, in many cases of people being physically healed. It is also used of a person being delivered from demons and of a dead person being brought back to life. In the case of Lazarus, it is used of recovering from a fatal illness. In 2 Timothy 4:18 Paul uses the same verb to describe God's on-going preservation and protection from evil, which will extend throughout his life.

The total outworking of salvation includes every part of a person's being. It is beautifully summed up in Paul's prayer in 1 Thessalonians 5:23: "Now may the

God of peace Himself sanctify you completely; and may your whole spirit, soul and body be preserved blameless at the coming of our Lord Jesus Christ." Salvation includes the total human personality — spirit, soul and body — and it is consummated only by the resurrection of the body at the return of Christ.

Nobody enters into all the various provisions of salvation all at once. It is normal to progress from one stage of provision to the next. Many Christians never get beyond receiving the forgiveness of their sins. They are not aware of the many other provisions that are freely available to them.

The order in which a person receives the various provisions is determined by the sovereignty of God, who deals with all of us as individuals. He knows what our greatest need is at any given time even if we ourselves are not aware of it. God sets a choice before each of us. The alternatives are clear: life and blessings, on the one hand; death and curses on the other. Like Israel, we determine our destiny by the choice we make. Our choice may also affect the destiny of our descendants.

Once we have made this choice, we can go on to claim release from any curses over our lives. What are the steps that we must take for this? There is no one set pattern that everyone must follow. In bringing people to the point of release, however, I have found it useful to lead them through the seven steps outlined below.

1. Confess your faith in Christ and His sacrifice on your behalf.

In Romans 10:9-10 Paul explains that there are two essential conditions for receiving the benefits of Christ's sacrifice: to *believe* in the heart that God raised Jesus from the dead and to *confess* with the mouth that He is Lord. Faith in the heart is not fully effective until it has been completed by confession with the mouth.

Literally, the word *confess* means "to say the same as." In the context of biblical faith, *confession* means saying with our mouth what God has already said in His Word. In Hebrews 3:1 Jesus is called "the High Priest of our confession." When we make the right scriptural confession concerning Him, it releases His priestly ministry on our behalf.

2. Repent of all your rebellion and sin.

You must accept personal responsibility for your rebellious attitude toward God and the sins that have resulted from it. Here is a suggested confession that expresses the repentance that God demands:

I give up all my rebellion and all my sin
and I submit myself to You as Lord.

3. Receive forgiveness of all sins.

The great barrier that keeps God's blessing out of our lives is *unforgiven sin*. God has already made provision for our sins to be forgiven, but He will not do this until we confess them. It may be that God has shown you certain sins that opened you up to a curse. If so, make a specific confession of those sins. "*If we confess our sins*, He is faithful and just to forgive us our sins and to cleanse us from all unrighteousness" (1 John 1:9).

4. Forgive all other people who have ever harmed you or wronged you.

Another great barrier that can keep God's blessing out of our lives is *unforgiveness* in our hearts toward other people. Forgiving another person is not primarily an emotion; it is a decision. Ask God to bring to mind anyone you need to forgive. The Holy Spirit will prompt you to make the right decision, but He will not make it for you. Say out loud, "Lord, I forgive _____."

5. Renounce all contact with occult or satanic things.

This includes a very wide range of activities and practices. If you have been involved at any time in such activities and practices, you have crossed an invisible border into the kingdom of Satan. Since that time, whether you know it or not, Satan has regarded you as one of his subjects. He considers that he has a legal claim to you.

"You need to finally and forever cut off all connection with Satan."

You need to finally and forever cut off all connection with Satan. If you are unsure about any particular activity, ask God to make it clear to you. You also need to get rid of all objects that could still link you with any of the above activities. This includes all images, charms, books etc. They should be burned or smashed or otherwise destroyed.

6. You are now ready to pray the prayer of release from any curse.

It is important that you base your faith solely upon what Jesus obtained for you through His sacrifice on the cross. You do not have to "earn" your release. You do not have to be "worthy".

Here is a prayer that would be appropriate:

> *Lord Jesus Christ, I believe that You are the Son of God and the only way to God; and that You died on the cross for my sins and rose again from the dead.*
>
> *I give up all my rebellion and all my sin and I submit myself to You as my Lord.*
>
> *I confess all my sins before You and ask You for Your forgiveness — especially for any sins that have exposed me to a curse. Release me also from the consequences of my ancestors' sins.*
>
> *By a decision of my will, I forgive all who have harmed or wronged me — just as I want God to forgive me. In particular, I forgive...*
>
> *I renounce all contact with anything*

occult or satanic — if I have any "contact objects", I commit myself to destroy them. I cancel all Satan's claims against me.

Lord Jesus, I believe that on the cross You took on Yourself every curse that could ever come upon me. So I ask You now to release me from every curse over my life — in Your name, Lord Jesus Christ!

By faith I now receive my release and I thank You for it.

7. Now believe that you have received and go on in God's blessing!

Do not try at this stage to analyze what form the blessing will take or how God will impart it to you. Leave that in God's hands. Let Him do it just how and when He will. You do not have to concern yourself with that. Your part is simply to open yourself, without reservation, to all that God wants to do in you and for you through His blessing. It will be exciting to see just how God will respond!

09 | From Shadows to Sunlight

If you followed the instructions in the previous chapter, you have crossed an invisible boundary. Behind you now is a territory overshadowed by curses of many different kinds and from many different sources. Before you lies a territory made bright by the sunshine of God's blessings.

You have an inheritance in Christ that is waiting to be explored and claimed. Look again at the summary of the blessings Moses gave in Deuteronomy 28:2-13:

- **exaltation**
- **health**
- **reproductiveness**
- **prosperity**
- **victory**
- **God's favour**

As you repeat these words, ask God to make this inheritance real and vivid to you. Giving thanks to God for each part is the purest and simplest expression of faith. If you have had a long struggle with a curse over your life, there may be areas of your mind from which the darkness is not immediately dispelled. Repeating these positive words that describe the blessings will be like seeing the first rays of the sun shining into a dark valley, then spreading to illuminate the whole valley.

> *"...the blessing comes only in Christ Jesus. It cannot be earned on our own merits."*

The transition from the dark to the sunlit territory may take many different forms. There is no single pattern that is standard for everyone. Some people experience almost instantaneous release and seem to enter immediately into the blessings that Scripture promises. For others, who are equally sincere, there may be a long hard struggle, especially if they have been deeply involved with the occult.

God's perspective is different from ours. In His sovereignty He takes into account factors in a situation about which we know nothing. He always keeps His promises, but in most cases there are two things He does not reveal in advance: the precise way that He will work in each life, and the precise time He will take.

We need to look once more at the positive side of the exchange described by Paul in

Galatians 3:13-14:

> *Christ has redeemed us from the curse*
> *of the law, having become a curse for*
> *us (for it is written, "Cursed is everyone*
> *who hangs on a tree"), that the blessing of*
> *Abraham might come upon the Gentiles*
> *in Christ Jesus, that we might receive the*
> *promise of the Spirit through faith.*

Paul points out three important facts concerning the promised blessing. First, it is not something vague or undefined. It is quite specific: the blessings of Abraham in Genesis 24:1. Its extent is defined: "The Lord had blessed Abraham in *all* things".

Second, the blessing comes only in Christ Jesus. It cannot be earned on our own merits. It is offered solely on the basis of relationship to God through Jesus Christ.

Third, the blessing is further defined as "the promise of the [Holy] Spirit." All three persons of the Godhead — Father, Son and Holy Spirit — are united in their purpose to share with us all that has been purchased for us by the sacrifice of Jesus. Because this is far greater than the natural mind can comprehend, we must depend on the Holy Spirit to guide us into our full inheritance and to show us how to appropriate what God has provided for us.

In Romans 8:14 Paul emphasizes the unique role of the Holy Spirit: "For as many as are led by the Spirit of God, these are sons of God." To be "led by the Holy Spirit" is not a single, once-for-all experience. It is something we must depend on moment by moment as we grow into maturity.

The Holy Spirit gives discernment of the causes of spiritual blockages and obedience to subsequent guidance is always a vital factor in moving effectively in the spiritual dimension. In the East Malaysian state of Sarawak, the Iban people are the majority ethnic group of the region and their culture is strongly influenced by animistic practices, including curses and the use of ancestral charms for protection and working spells. The message of freedom from bondage to such things is currently having a dramatic impact among them. In a number of villages, as the message has been preached, there has been a lot of confession and repentance and many have been delivered from evil spirits as they have been prayed for. In each place a large sack of *jimats* (ancestral charms) was collected which were all burnt.

In one place however, even after doing that, it was felt that there was still a stronghold in the longhouse which had not been properly dealt with. The Holy Spirit prompted them to have what they called a "Jericho march" around the longhouse where they were. Exactly on the seventh time round the leader shouted, "Stop!" Immediately a charm which they had overlooked, crashed to the floor and this turned out to be the most powerful charm in the village. After they burnt this as well, there was tremendous peace and joy that came over the people.

This same peace and joy can be yours as you learn to walk in obedience to the Holy Spirit and learn to speak out the promises of God's Word with confidence. In the prayer of release in chapter 8, the initial focus is on the truth revealed in Hebrews 3:1: Jesus is "the High Priest of our confession." This principle should also govern our on-going relationship with the Lord. In every situation we encounter, we must respond with an appropriate scriptural confession in order to invoke the continuing ministry of Jesus as our High Priest.

In most situations we have three possible ways to respond: to make a positive, scriptural confession; to make no confession; to make a negative, unscriptural confession. If we make a positive confession, we release the ministry of Jesus to help us and to meet our need. If we make no confession, we are left at the mercy of our circumstances. If we make a negative confession, we expose ourselves to evil, demonic forces.

It is important to distinguish between the scriptural confession of genuine faith and such things as wishful thinking. Firstly, "confession" in

"It implies a transition from a defensive posture to one of attack."

the biblical sense is limited to the statements and promises of the Bible. Beyond this we cannot go. Secondly, confession is only valid if we fulfil the appropriate conditions attached to the promise. It is never a substitute for obedience. Thirdly, confession cannot be reduced to a convenient "system" or "formula", operated by human will or mental faith. We cannot manipulate God. Genuine faith in the heart is produced only by the Holy Spirit, and it produces *words charged with power* to accomplish what is confessed. Hebrews 10:23 encourages us to persevere in our confession: "Let us hold fast the confession of our hope without wavering, for He who promised is faithful."

To give full, victorious expression to faith, however, there is one further biblical concept that takes us beyond confession. It is "proclamation". This suggests a strong, confident assertion of faith, which cannot be silenced by any form of opposition or discouragement. It implies a transition from a defensive posture to one of *attack*.

In ministry Ruth and I are often asked how we protect ourselves on a daily basis. We make a regular practice of proclaiming God's Word out loud, alone or together. On the following pages is a declaration that we make every night before we go to sleep. We would like to recommend that you do this too, so that you may also pass from shadows to sunlight, from curse into the fullness of God's blessing.

Declaration of Confidence in God's Protection

No weapon that is formed against me shall prosper and every tongue that arises against me in judgment I do condemn. This is my heritage as a servant of the Lord and my righteousness is from You, O Lord of Hosts.

If there are those who have been speaking or praying against me, or seeking to harm me, or who have rejected me, I forgive them (name people if you know them). Having forgiven them, I bless them in the name of the Lord.[1]

Now I declare, O Lord, that You and You alone are my God. Besides You there is no other; a just God and a Saviour; the Father, Son and Spirit and I worship You!

I submit myself afresh to You today in unreserved obedience. Having submitted to You, Lord, I do as Your Word directs. I resist the devil: all his pressures, his attacks, his deceptions and every instrument or agent he would seek to use against me. I do not submit! I resist him, drive him from me and exclude him from me in the name of Jesus.

Specifically I resist and repel: infirmity, infection, pain, inflammation, malignancies, allergies, viruses, _____[2] every form of witchcraft and every type of stress.

Finally, Lord, I thank You that through the sacrifice of Jesus on the cross, I have passed out from under the curse and entered into the blessing of Abraham whom You blessed in all things: exaltation, health, prosperity, reproductiveness, victory, God's favour and God's friendship.[3]

Amen.

1. See Matthew 5:43-45, Romans 12:14
2. Name any other sickness or spirits which you feel have been coming against you.
3. See Galatians 3:13-14, Genesis 24:1

Further Study

• Blessing or Curse: You Can Choose!

[B56 - Book]

Blessings and curses are two of the most powerful forces shaping your destiny—for good or for evil. Derek Prince reveals, from Scripture and personal experience, how to recognize a curse at work and how to pass from curse to blessing. (372 pp)

• Release from the Curse

[4285/4286 - Audio cassette or CD]

[V4285/V4286 - Video]

[D4285/D4286 - DVD]

• Curses: Cause and Cure

[6011 - Curses: Cause]

[6012 - Curses: Cure, Part 1]

[6013 - Curses: Cure, Part 2]

[CC1 - Set of 3 audio cassettes or CDs]

Many people experience continual frustration in areas such as marriage, health or finances, yet never discern the underlying cause: a curse. This series reveals both cause and cure.

For a full resource guide of Derek Prince DVDs and CDs, please contact the DPM office nearest you (see pg 107-108 for office addresses).

About the Author

Derek Prince (1915–2003) was born in India of British parents. Educated as a scholar of Greek and Latin at Eton College and Cambridge University, England, he held a Fellowship in Ancient and Modern Philosophy at King's College. He also studied several modern languages, including Hebrew and Aramaic, at Cambridge University and the Hebrew University in Jerusalem.

While serving with the British army in World War II, he began to study the Bible and experienced a life-changing encounter with Jesus Christ. Out of this encounter he formed two conclusions: first, that Jesus Christ is alive; second, that the Bible is a true, relevant, up-to-date book. These conclusions altered the whole course of his life, which he then devoted to studying and teaching the Bible.

Derek's main gift of explaining the Bible and its teaching in a clear and simple way has helped build a foundation of faith in millions of lives. His non-denominational, non-sectarian approach has made his teaching equally relevant and helpful to people from all racial and religious backgrounds.

He is the author of over 50 books, 600 audio and 100 video teachings, many of which have been translated and published in more than 100 languages. His daily radio broadcast is translated into Arabic, Chinese (Amoy, Cantonese, Mandarin, Shanghaiese, Swatow), Croatian, German, Malagasy, Mongolian, Russian, Samoan, Spanish, Bahasa Indonesian and Tongan. The radio program continues to touch lives around the world.

Derek Prince Ministries continues its ministry of reaching out to believers in over 140 countries with Derek's teachings, fulfilling the mandate to keep on "until Jesus returns". This is effected through the outreaches of more than 30 Derek Prince Offices around the world, including primary work in Australia, Canada, China, France, Germany, the Netherlands, New Zealand, Norway, Russia, South Africa, Switzerland, the United Kingdom and the United States. For current information about these and other worldwide locations, visit www.derekprince.com.

Books by Derek Prince

Appointment in Jerusalem
At the End of Time *
Authority and Power of God's Word *
Be Perfect
Blessing or Curse: You Can Choose
Bought With Blood
By Grace Alone
Called to Conquer
Choice of a Partner, The
Complete Salvation
Declaring God's Word
Derek Prince—A Biography by Stephen Mansfield
Derek Prince: On Experiencing God's Power
Destiny Of Israel and The Church, The
Divine Exchange, The
Doctrine of Baptisms, The *
Does Your Tongue Need Healing?
End of Life's Journey, The
Entering the Presence of God
Expelling Demons
Explaining Blessings and Curses
Extravagant Love
Faith and Works *
Faith to Live By
Fasting
Final Judgment *
First Mile, The
Foundational Truths For Christian Living
Founded On the Rock *
Gifts of the Spirit, The
God Is a Matchmaker
God's Medicine Bottle
God's Plan for Your Money
God's Remedy for Rejection
God's Will for Your Life
God's Word Heals
Grace of Yielding, The
Harvest Just Ahead, The
Holy Spirit in You, The
How to Fast Successfully
Husbands and Fathers
I Forgive You
Immersion in The Spirit *
Judging
Key to the Middle East
Laying the Foundations Series*
Life's Bitter Pool
Life Changing Spiritual Power
Living As Salt and Light
Lucifer Exposed
Marriage Covenant, The
Orphans, Widows, the Poor and Oppressed
Our Debt to Israel
Pages from My Life's Book
Partners for Life
Philosophy, the Bible and the Supernatural

Power in the Name
Power of the Sacrifice, The
Prayers and Proclamations
Praying for the Government
Promise of Provision, The
Prophetic Guide to the End
    Times
Protection from Deception
Pulling Down Strongholds
Receiving God's Best
Rediscovering God's Church
Resurrection of the Body *
Rules of Engagement
Secrets of a Prayer Warrior
Self-Study Bible Course
    (revised and expanded)
Set Apart For God
Shaping History Through
    Prayer and Fasting

Spiritual Warfare
Surviving the Last Days
Thanksgiving, Praise and
    Worship
They Shall Expel Demons
Through Repentance to
    Faith *
Through the Psalms with
    Derek Prince
Transmitting God's Power *
The Two Harvests
Three Messages For Israel
War in Heaven
Where Wisdom Begins
Who Is the Holy Spirit?
Will You Intercede?
You Matter to God
You Shall Receive Power

*Foundations Series

1. Founded on the Rock (B100)
2. Authority and Power of God's Word (B101)
3. Through Repentance to Faith (B102)
4. Faith and Works (B103)
5. The Doctrine of Baptisms (B104)
6. Immersion in The Spirit (B105)
7. Transmitting God's Power (B106)
8. At the End of Time (B107)
9. Resurrection of the Body (B108)
10. Final Judgment (B109)

DPM Offices

For further information about Derek Prince Ministries or to obtain Derek's teaching materials, please contact your nearest DPM office.

DPM-ASIA/PACIFIC
PO Box 2029
Christchurch 8140
NEW ZEALAND
Ph: 0064 3 366 4443
Fax: 0064 3 366 1569
Email: admin@dpm.co.nz
www.derekprince.co.nz

DPM-AUSTRALIA
1st Floor, 134 Pendle Way
Pendle Hill
New South Wales 2145
AUSTRALIA
Ph: 0061 2 9688 4488
Fax: 0061 2 9688 4848
Email:
enquiries@au.derekprince.com

DPM-CANADA
P.O. Box 8354
Halifax, N.S. B3K 5M1
Canada
Ph: + 1 902 443 9577
Fax: + 1 902 443 6013
E-mail: enquiries.dpm@eastlink.ca

DPM-INDIA
No. 1C, E.V.R. Rd, 2nd & 3rd Flrs
Opp. Chinthamani Mall
Puthur
Trichy 620 017
Tamil Nadu
INDIA
Ph: +91 958 5538 201/02/03
Email: admin@derekprince.in
www.derekprince.in

DPM-MALAYSIA
Ph: 0060 3 4251 6882
Email: ygmdpm@streamyx.com

DPM-MYANMAR
Email: dprincemm@gmail.com

DPM-NEPAL
C/o The Lord's Assembly
P O Box 1083
Kathmadu, Nepal
Ph: 009771 411 1729
Fax: 009771 410 60866
Email: goodnews@enet.com.np

DPM-PAKISTAN
Email: dpmpak@khi.comsats.
net.pk

DPM-SOUTH AFRICA
PO Box 33367
Glenstantia 0010
Pretoria
SOUTH AFRICA
Ph: 0027 12 348 9537
Fax: 0027 12 348 9538
Email: dpmsa@mweb.co.za

DPM-UNITED KINGDOM
Kingsfield, Hadrian Way
Baldock, SG7 6AN
ENGLAND
Ph: 44-1462-492100
Fax: 44-1462-492102
Email: enquiries@dpmuk.org

DPM-USA
P. O. Box 19501
Charlotte
NC 28219-9501
USA
Ph: 704-357-3556
Fax: 704-357-1413
Email:
contactus@derekprince.org
www.derekprince.org

West Africa is currently under the auspices of the DPM-UK office.